MW01108921

DECEMBER

The
Birthstone Petite
Collection

By Suzanne Siegel Zenkel

Design and illustration by
Mullen and Katz

PETER PAUPER PRESS, INC.
WHITE PLAINS · NEW YORK

Special thanks to
Lois L. Kaufman and
Claudine Gandolfi for their
editorial assistance

Copyright © 1996
Peter Pauper Press, Inc.
202 Mamaroneck Avenue
White Plains, NY 10601
ISBN 0-88088-986-1
Printed in China
7 6 5 4 3 2 1

Contents

December
A Month Like No Other

———

YOUR BIRTHSTONES ARE THE
Turquoise AND THE *Zircon*

AND YOUR SPECIAL FLOWER IS THE
Poinsettia

*God gave us memory
so that we might have roses
in December.*

J. M. BARRIE

*I heard the bells on Christmas day
Their old, familiar carols play,
And wild and sweet
The words repeat
Of peace on earth, good will to men.*

HENRY WADSWORTH LONGFELLOW

Peace on Earth! No three words better capture the feel of December—that magical month when holiday cheer warms the frosty air and fills our hearts with kindness.

Named for the Latin word meaning "ten," December was the tenth month in the ancient Roman calendar. When Julius Caesar reformed the calendar, it became the twelfth and last month of the year. But last is certainly not least in the case of wondrous December, where good will overflows throughout its thirty-one days.

December ushers in Old Man Winter, with the Old Man at his jolliest! On the 21st or 22nd day of the month, the Winter solstice occurs, officially beginning the season. It is the shortest day of the year, when day's light is at its minimum. Folks have humorously dubbed it "National Flashlight Day," because it marks the night "when people could use a flashlight the most!" But for spirited December lovers, the first long day of Winter is a splendid occasion for gathering 'round a crackling fire and stoking its brilliant flames.

Of course the Holidays provide the most marvelous occasions for December gatherings! On the 25th, celebrations abound to commemorate the birth of Jesus Christ—with the warmth and joy of mistletoe, lights, holly and ivy, caroling, and gift-giving. The Jewish festival of Hanukah usually falls in the month of December as well. This eight day Festival of Lights commemorates the victory of the Maccabees over the Syrians in 165 B.C. and the rededication of the Temple of

Jerusalem. December also hosts a secular celebration of immense proportions—New Year's Eve! People the world over make resolutions on December 31st, and usher in the New Year with all kinds of festivities and revelry. The fanfare customarily involves fireworks, a countdown led by the lighted "Big Apple" in Times Square, and music, including the favorite Scottish tribute to the good old days, now an American tradition, *Auld Lang Syne*.

December is special not only for its indomitable holiday spirit, but for its roster of important historical events. The Bill of Rights was ratified on December 15, 1791, for one. These first ten amendments to the U.S. Constitution provide protection for freedom of speech, religion, assembly, and the press. They also restrict the government's rights of search and seizure, and list distinct rights of people accused of crimes. Annually, December 15th marks Bill of Rights Day, honoring the ratification anniversary. On December 18, 1865, the 13th Amendment to the U.S. Constitution was proclaimed, putting an end to slavery, freeing our Nation from its oppression: "Neither slavery nor involuntary servitude . . . shall exist within the United States, or any place subject to their jurisdiction."

And Americans were flying high when the Wright brothers made their first successful powered and controlled flight in an airplane! After three years of experimentation with kites and gliders, Orville Wright piloted history's first airplane on December 17, 1903. The flight lasted for less than one minute, but it opened the skies to unlimited new heights in the world of aviation.

The sky's indeed the limit for interesting December happenings. In December, 1929, the innovative Edwin S. Lowe first manufactured the game of Bingo, which players of all ages have been enjoying ever since. And December marks the birth of America's most famous soap, Ivory. Invented accidentally by Harley Procter and his cousin, Gamble, the soap's name was inspired by a reference to ivory

palaces in the 45th Psalm. After naming his buoyant bath bar, Mr. Procter sent samples off to chemists in December, 1882. Pure and dependable Ivory Soap has been an American favorite ever since the idea was first floated!

Now delight in the spirit of the season as you turn the pages and discover who shares your glorious birth month. And may your days be merry and bright—filled with all the cheer and good will that the month of December inspires!

December Celebrities and What They Have to Say

December 1

REX STOUT, 1886

MARY MARTIN, 1913

DICK SHAWN, 1923

December 1

Life. Full of loneliness and misery
and suffering and unhappiness, and
it's all over much too quickly.

WOODY ALLEN, 1935

LOU RAWLS, 1936
LEE TREVINO, 1939
RICHARD PRYOR, 1940

After thirty,
a body has a mind of its own.

BETTE MIDLER, 1944

December 1

CAROL ALT, 1960

December 2

ALEXANDER HAIG, JR., 1924

JULIE HARRIS, 1925

WILLIAM WEGMAN, 1943

RANDY GARDNER, 1958

MONICA SELES, 1973

December 3

GILBERT STUART, 1755

FERLIN HUSKY, 1927

ANDY WILLIAMS, 1930

JAYE P. MORGAN, 1932

BOBBY ALLISON, 1937

RICK MEARS, 1951

DARYL HANNAH, 1961

December 4

LILLIAN RUSSELL, 1861

RAINER MARIA RILKE, 1875

DEANNA DURBIN, 1921

DENNIS WILSON, 1944

JEFF BRIDGES, 1949

MARISA TOMEI, 1964

December 5

Better by far
that you should forget and smile
than that you should remember
and be sad.

CHRISTINA ROSSETTI, 1830

There's nothing funnier than
the human animal.

WALT DISNEY, 1901

OTTO PREMINGER, 1906
JOAN DIDION, 1934

December 5

CALVIN TRILLIN, 1935

CHAD MITCHELL, 1936

MORGAN BRITTANY, 1950

CARRIE HAMILTON, 1963

December 6

Joyce Kilmer, 1886

Lynn Fontanne, 1892

Ira Gershwin, 1896

Alfred Eisenstaedt, 1898

Agnes Moorehead, 1906

Dave Brubeck, 1920

Tom Hulce, 1953

December 7

MARY, QUEEN OF SCOTS, 1542
MADAME MARIE TUSSAUD, 1761

Nothing really matters but living—
accomplishments are the ornaments
of life, they come second.

WILLA CATHER, 1873

December 7

JOYCE CARY, 1888

ELI WALLACH, 1915

TED KNIGHT, 1923

ELLEN BURSTYN, 1932

GREG ALLMAN, 1947

JOHNNY BENCH, 1947

LARRY BIRD, 1956

December 8

HORACE, 65 B.C.

CHRISTINA,
QUEEN OF SWEDEN, 1626

ELI WHITNEY, 1765

DIEGO RIVERA, 1886

I'm 65 and I guess that puts me in
with the geriatrics. But if there were
fifteen months in every year, I'd
only be 48. That's the trouble with
us. We number everything.

JAMES THURBER, 1894

December 8

LEE J. COBB, 1911

SAMMY DAVIS, JR., 1925

FLIP WILSON, 1933

DAVID CARRADINE, 1936

JAMES GALWAY, 1939

JIM MORRISON, 1943

KIM BASINGER, 1953

December 9

HERMIONE GINGOLD, 1897
EMMETT KELLY, 1898
DOUGLAS FAIRBANKS, JR., 1909
THOMAS P. O'NEILL, 1912

I have lasted more than forty years
in Hollywood, where stars come
and go. Not bad for the ragman's
son. All my life, I always knew I
would be somebody.

KIRK DOUGLAS, 1916

December 9

Redd Foxx, 1922

Dina Merrill, 1925

Dick Van Patten, 1928

Beau Bridges, 1941

Joan Armatrading, 1950

John Malkovich, 1953

Donny Osmond, 1957

December 10

THOMAS HOPKINS
GALLAUDET, 1787
EMILY DICKINSON, 1830
MELVIL DEWEY, 1851

CHET HUNTLEY, 1911
DOROTHY LAMOUR, 1914
GLORIA LORING, 1946
SUSAN DEY, 1952
KENNETH BRANAGH, 1960

December 11

FIORELLO H. LA GUARDIA, 1882
CARLO PONTI, 1913

Life is there, beneath the chaos.
It is moving forward. Green shoots
are pushing up again through
the waste. There is hope.

ALEKSANDR SOLZHENITSYN, 1918

RITA MORENO, 1931
DONNA MILLS, 1943

December 11

BRENDA LEE, 1944

LYNDA DAY GEORGE, 1946

TERRI GARR, 1949

BESS ARMSTRONG, 1951

SUSAN SEIDELMAN, 1952

JERMAINE JACKSON, 1954

December 12

JOHN JAY, 1745
GUSTAVE FLAUBERT, 1821
EDWARD G. ROBINSON, 1893

I adore making records. I'd rather
do that than almost anything else.
You can never do anything in life
quite on your own—you don't live
on your own little island. . . . But
once you're on that record singing,
it's you and you alone.

FRANK SINATRA, 1915

December 12

Bob Barker, 1923

Edward I. Koch, 1924

Helen Frankenthaler, 1928

Connie Francis, 1938

Dionne Warwick, 1941

Grover Washington, 1943

Cathy Rigby, 1952

December 13

MARY TODD LINCOLN, 1818
ALVIN "SERGEANT" YORK, 1887

VAN HEFLIN, 1910
DICK VAN DYKE, 1925
CHRISTOPHER PLUMMER, 1927
JOHN DAVIDSON, 1941
FERGUSON JENKINS, 1943

December 14

MARGARET CHASE SMITH, 1897

SPIKE JONES, 1911

MOREY AMSTERDAM, 1914

SHIRLEY JACKSON, 1919

CHARLIE RICH, 1932

LEE REMICK, 1935

December 14

I have horrible times, I have great
times, I have so-so times, but
I wouldn't trade my life today for
anyone's, not anyone's.
I've survived. I've beaten my
own bad system and on some
days, on most days, that feels
like a miracle.

PATTY DUKE, 1946

STAN SMITH, 1946

December 15

ALEXANDRE EIFFEL, 1832

MAXWELL ANDERSON, 1888

JEAN PAUL GETTY, 1892

EDNA O'BRIEN, 1930

TIM CONWAY, 1933

DON JOHNSON, 1949

HELEN SLATER, 1965

December 16

LUDWIG VAN BEETHOVEN, 1770
JANE AUSTEN, 1775

Try to find something that needs to
be done that only you can do.

MARGARET MEAD, 1901

ARTHUR C. CLARKE, 1917
LIV ULLMANN, 1939
LESLEY STAHL, 1941
STEVEN BOCHCO, 1943

December 17

ARTHUR FIEDLER, 1894
ERSKINE CALDWELL, 1903
GENE RAYBURN, 1917
WILLIAM SAFIRE, 1929
TOMMY STEELE, 1936
EUGENE LEVY, 1946

December 18

TY COBB, 1886
BETTY GRABLE, 1916
OSSIE DAVIS, 1917

December 18

ROGER SMITH, 1932

Wait until you get our age
and see how you run.

KEITH RICHARDS, 1943

I am a cinematic. I'm scared to
death of the dark—except in a
movie theater.

STEVEN SPIELBERG, 1947

JANIE FRICKIE, 1950
LEONARD MALTIN, 1950

December 19

SIR RALPH RICHARDSON, 1902

BOBBY LAYNE, 1926

CICELY TYSON, 1933

AL KALINE, 1934

ROBERT URICH, 1946

December 20

BRANCH RICKEY, 1881

IRENE DUNNE, 1898

GEORGE ROY HILL, 1922

JOHN HILLERMAN, 1932

JENNY AGUTTER, 1952

December 21

PAUL WINCHELL, 1922

PHIL DONAHUE, 1935

JANE FONDA, 1937

CHRIS EVERT, 1954

FLORENCE GRIFFITH
JOYNER, 1959

December 22

GIACOMO PUCCINI, 1858

LADY BIRD JOHNSON, 1912

BARBARA BILLINGSLEY, 1922

STEVE CARLTON, 1944

DIANE SAWYER, 1945

December 23

JOSEPH SMITH, 1805

YOUSUF KARSH, 1908

JOSE GRECO, 1918

RUTH ROMAN, 1923

SUSAN LUCCI, 1949

December 24

KIT CARSON, 1809
HOWARD HUGHES, 1905

I've had a hell of a good time,
so my face looks, well, lived-in.
You won't find me standing in fron
of a mirror, weeping.

AVA GARDNER, 1922

JILL BENNETT. 1931
MARY HIGGINS CLARK, 1931
NICHOLAS MEYER, 1945

December 25

CLARA BARTON, 1821

EVANGELINE BOOTH, 1865

REBECCA WEST, 1892

HUMPHREY BOGART, 1899

CAB CALLOWAY, 1907

Remember: The grass may look
greener on the other side,
but it's just as hard to cut.

LITTLE RICHARD, 1935

December 25

I am a Christian, so having my birthday on December 25, the same day we celebrate our Savior, Jesus Christ's birth, is most special to me.

BARBARA MANDRELL, 1948

JIMMY BUFFETT, 1946

SISSY SPACEK, 1949

ANNIE LENNOX, 1954

December 26

RICHARD WIDMARK, 1914

STEVE ALLEN, 1921

DORIS LILLY, 1926

ALAN KING, 1927

SUSAN BUTCHER, 1954

December 27

LOUIS PASTEUR, 1822

SYDNEY GREENSTREET, 1879

MARLENE DIETRICH, 1901

December 27

BERNARD LANVIN, 1935

COKIE ROBERTS, 1943

TRACY NELSON, 1944

At twenty you have many desires
which hide the truth, but beyond
forty there are only real and
fragile truths—your abilities
and your failings.

GÉRARD DEPARDIEU, 1948

TOVAH FELDSHUH, 1952

December 28

WOODROW WILSON, 1856
CLIFF ARQUETTE, 1904
EARL "FATHA" HINES, 1905
SAM LEVENSON, 1911
HILDEGARDE NEFF, 1925
MAGGIE SMITH, 1934

My mother helped over the years by
telling me, "It ain't brain surgery
that you're doing."
DENZEL WASHINGTON, 1954

December 29

ANDREW JOHNSON, 1808

If you continue to work and
absorb the beauty in the world, you
find that age does not necessarily
mean getting old.

PABLO CASALS, 1876

VIVECA LINDFORS, 1920
MARY TYLER MOORE, 1937
JON VOIGHT, 1938
MARIANNE FAITHFULL, 1946
TED DANSON, 1947

Parties, Cakes, Candles, Flowers, and Birthstones

Happy Birthday to You

It should come as no surprise that *Happy Birthday to You* is commonly referred to as "the most frequently sung number in the world." After all, a birthday is one of the few things in life that we all have.

Birthdays mean different things to each of us. When we were children, most of us regarded our birthday with boundless excitement, reveling in our chance to be the focus of attention. To adults, birthdays evoke an enormous range of sentiments, awakening for some of us excitement reminiscent of childhood. Others spend their birthdays reflecting on the events of the passing years or anticipating what the future holds. Yet, no matter how we regard our birthday at a given time, we all feel a certain response to the day. And from time immemorial, one of the very best ways to celebrate a birthday has been to throw a party and have a ball!

Life's a Party

How did birthday parties come to be? The first to throw birthday parties were the ancient Europeans. In those days, people believed strongly in the power of good and evil spirits, and how the evil spirits might prey on a birthday celebrant was unknown. Family and friends would gather 'round the celebrant in order to ward off any evil spirits. Thus, the origins of the first birthday party, replete with good wishes and cheer, were thought to be to protect the celebrant from any mysterious dangers a birthday might present.

Birthday gifts were believed to offer even greater protection from evil spirits. People also reveled in games and fun as a symbol of bidding farewell to the past year and bringing in the new year with joy. In the earliest days, birthday parties were planned for only the most prominent in the community. As time evolved, the custom was shared by common people and eventually children's birthdays became the most celebrated of all. So, birthday parties were first fashioned in order to assure the next year's good fortune.

Have Your Cake and Eat It, Too!

Who first cooked up the idea of a birthday cake? The ancient Greeks believed in Artemis, Goddess of the Moon. In celebration of her birthday, they would bring round, moon-shaped cakes to her temple. Birthday cakes are often round, reminiscent of this custom. In the United States, there has evolved another tradition—that of having the celebrant cut the first slice.

Don't Burn the Candle at Both Ends!

Why the old flame at your birthday party? The first to use lighted candles on birthday cakes were the Germans. The birthday celebrant silently made a wish and then blew out the flames. The wish would be granted only if all the candles were blown out in one puff. The custom to have one candle for each year evolved from this tradition, and in the United States and elsewhere, one candle "to grow on" has been added.

Older Grown

The days are gone,
The months have flown,
And you and I are older grown.
Shake hands, good-bye,
and have no fear
To welcome well another year.

KATE GREENAWAY

Say It with Flowers!

Each month has a special flower associated with it.

Month	Flower
JANUARY	CARNATION
FEBRUARY	PRIMROSE
MARCH	DAFFODIL
APRIL	DAISY
MAY	LILY OF THE VALLEY
JUNE	ROSE
JULY	LARKSPUR
AUGUST	GLADIOLUS
SEPTEMBER	ASTER
OCTOBER	DAHLIA
NOVEMBER	CHRYSANTHEMUM
DECEMBER	POINSETTIA

You're a Gem!

The most widely embraced of the customs associated with birthdays is the wearing of the birthstone—the gemstone which symbolizes the month of your birth. In ancient times, people believed that good luck would be brought to a person wearing his or her birthstone. Many also believed that wearing one's birthstone strengthened character. The following lists the gems generally accepted as the birthstone for each month.

Month	*Stone*
JANUARY	GARNET
FEBRUARY	AMETHYST
MARCH	AQUAMARINE
APRIL	DIAMOND
MAY	EMERALD
JUNE	PEARL
JULY	RUBY
AUGUST	PERIDOT
SEPTEMBER	SAPPHIRE
OCTOBER	TOURMALINE/OPAL
NOVEMBER	TOPAZ
DECEMBER	TURQUOISE/ZIRCON

Happy
Birthday
to You!